Web-Spinning Spiders

by Laura Hamilton Waxman

first step nonfiction

Lerner Publications ◆ Minneapolis

LERNER

SOURCE™

Expand learning beyond the printed book. Download free, complementary educational resources for this book from our website, www.lerneresource.com.

The images in this book are used with the permission of: © Katja Schulz/flickr (CC BY 2.0), p. 4; © iStockphoto/abzerit, p. 5; © USGS Bee Inventory and Monitoring Lab/flickr, p. 6; © Gido/flickr (CC BY 2.0), p. 7; © Glenda Christina/Design Pics/Corbis, p. 8; © Benny Mazur/flickr (CC BY 2.0), p. 9; © Gordon & Cathy Illg/Animals Animals, p. 10; Ivan Kuzmin imageBROKER/Newscom, p. 11; © Mark Chappell/Animals Animals, p. 12; © iStockphoto/Ichabod, p. 13; © BoldAngles.com/Shutterstock, p. 14; © NHPA/SuperStock, p. 15; © bobistraveling/flickr (CC BY 2.0), p. 16; CDC/James Gathany, p. 17; © John Lawlor/flickr (CC BY 2.0), p. 18; © Wonderlane/flickr (CC BY 2.0), p. 19; Darrell Gulin/Danita Delimont Photography/Newscom, p. 20; © Minden Pictures/SuperStock, p. 21; © Paul Marcellini (MYN)/Nature Picture Library/Corbis, p. 22. Front Cover: © Richard Gailey/flickr (CC BY 2.0).

Main body text set in ITC Avant Garde Gothic Std Medium 21/25.
Typeface provided by International Typeface Corp.

Lerner Publications Company
A division of Lerner Publishing Group, Inc.
241 First Avenue North
Minneapolis, MN 55401 USA

For reading levels and more information, look up this title at www.lernerbooks.com.

Library of Congress Cataloging-in-Publication Data

Names: Waxman, Laura Hamilton, author.
Title: Web-spinning spiders / by Laura Hamilton Waxman.
Description: Minneapolis, MN : Lerner Publications, [2016] | Series: First step nonfiction. Backyard critters | Audience: Ages 5–8. | Audience: K to grade 3. | Includes index.
Identifiers: LCCN 2015039106| ISBN 9781512408843 (lb : alk. paper) | ISBN 9781512412239 (pb : alk. paper) | ISBN 9781512410044 (eb pdf)
Subjects: LCSH: Spiders—Juvenile literature.
Classification: LCC QL458.4 .W39 2016 | DDC 595.4/4—dc23

LC record available at http://lccn.loc.gov/2015039106

Manufactured in the United States of America
1 – CG – 7/15/16

Table of Contents

Spider Bodies

A spider's body is made of two soft parts.

Eight long legs come out of the front part.

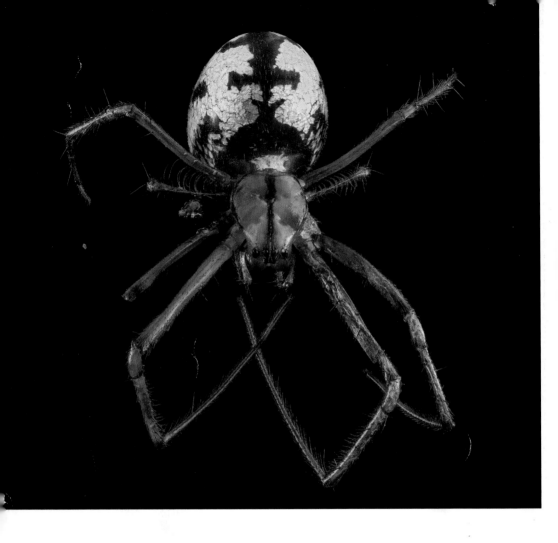

Each leg has six **joints** for
bending.

Spiders feel and smell
with their leg hairs.

The legs are covered with
tiny hairs.

Where to Find Spiders

Spiders live in almost every part of the world.

Some spiders can float!

They live in hot, cold, wet, and dry places.

They live wherever there is
enough food to eat.

Spiders mostly eat **insects**.

Spiders bite their food with
two **fangs**.

Most spider venom does not harm people.

Venom comes out of the fangs.

The venom **paralyzes** the food first. Then the food
turns into mush.

The spider sucks up its
mushy meal.

What Spiders Do

Spiders make **silk**.

It shoots out the back of
their bodies.

Webs can be shaped like circles, balls, lines, or tubes.

Spiders use silk to spin webs.

The webs are sticky and
hard to see.

Not all spiders make webs. Some chase their food on fast legs.

Insects fly into a web and get trapped.

Then the spider has a new meal!

Spider Parts

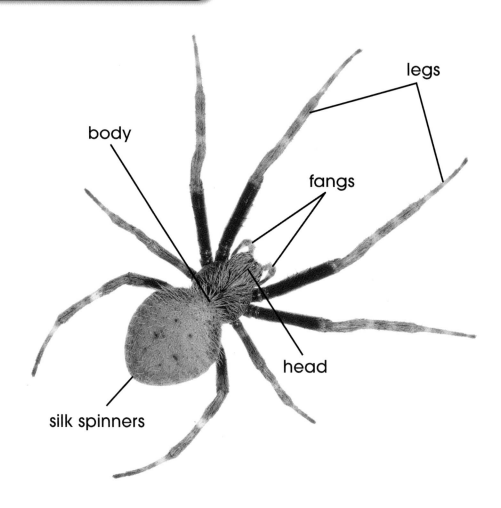

body

legs

fangs

head

silk spinners

Glossary

fangs – long, pointy teeth

insects – small animals with six legs

joints – places where two parts of an arm or a leg are joined together

paralyzes – makes someone or something unable to move

silk – thin, sticky thread

venom – something an animal makes to hurt or kill another animal

Index